Discover Innovation: The NUU Mobile A15 Smartphone Revealed

The Ultimate Guide to the A15 Android Smartphone

Paulson Witt

All rights reserved.

Without limiting the rights under copyright reserved above, no part of this publication may be reproduced, stored in or introduced into a database and retrieval system, or transmitted in any form or by any means (electronic, mechanical, photocopying, recording, or otherwise) without the prior written permission of both the owner of the copyright and the publishers mentioned above.

Copyright©2024 Paulson Witt

Disclaimer

The author of this book has nothing but good intentions, aiming to deliver valuable and useful information. Please note that certain images and text in this book were gathered from reliable sources and were not originally created by the author. However, rest assured that everything has been carefully examined and included with the reader's or user's benefit in mind. The main focus is on making this content as helpful as possible. Your understanding is greatly appreciated.

TABLE OF CONTENTS

- 1.0 Introduction 10
- 1.1 Why You Need to Choose the NUU A15 12
  - Unparalleled Design and Build Quality 12
    - Stunning Display 12
    - Powerful Performance 13
    - Ample Storage 13
    - Exceptional Camera System 14
    - Long-Lasting Battery 15
    - Advanced Connectivity 15
    - Enhanced User Experience 16
    - Security and Convenience 16
    - Excellent Value 17
- 2.0 Unboxing the NUU A15 18
  - 2.1 First Impressions 18
  - 2.2 What's in the Box? 19
- 3.0 Design and Build Quality 24
  - 3.1 Sleek and Sophisticated Aesthetics 24
  - 3.2 Minimalist and Ergonomic Design 25
  - 3.3 Robust Build Quality 26
  - 3.4 Premium Materials 26
  - 3.5 Thoughtful Details 27
  - 3.6 Display Excellence 28

3.7	Color Options: Dark Purple and Pure White	28
4.0	Display and Experience	30
4.1	Screen Specifications	30
4.2	Visual Clarity and Brightness	31
4.3	Touch Responsiveness	32
4.4	Immersive Viewing Experience	33
4.5	Adaptive Display Features	33
4.6	Eye Comfort Mode	34
5.0	Performance and Hardware	35
5.2	Internal Storage Options	36
5.3	Battery Life and Charging Speed	37
6.0	Software and User Interface	40
	Operating System Overview	40
6.1	Key Features and Customizations	41
	Expanded Themed App Icons	41
	Enhanced Media Experience	43
	Customizable Language Settings	44
	Privacy and Security Enhancements	45
	Pre-installed Applications	46
	Google Suite	46
	Essential Utilities	47
	NUU-Specific Applications	47
	Minimal Bloatware	48
7.0	Camera and Network	49

- 7.1. Camera Specifications 49
- 7.2 Photo and Video Quality...50
  - 7.2.1 Rear Camera Performance................................50
  - 7.2.2 Front Camera Performance...............................52
  - 7.2.3 Video Quality 52
- 7.3 Advanced Camera Features 53
  - **7.3.1** AI Camera Modes..53
  - 7.3.2 Pro Mode 54
  - 7.3.3 Selfie Enhancements 55
- 7.4 Network..56
  - 7.4.1 Connectivity Options..56
  - 7.4.2 Dual SIM Capability...57
  - 7.4.3 Expandable Storage..58
- 8.0 Audio and Multimedia 60
  - 8.1 Sound Quality and Speaker Performance 60
    - Sound Quality..60
    - Speaker Performance...60
  - 8.2 Media Playback Features 61
    - Enhanced Media Experience...61
    - Versatile Media Support..62
    - Streaming and Connectivity 63
    - Audio Enhancements and Customizations......................63
- 10.0 Security and Privacy 65
  - 10.1 Fingerprint Sensor and Face Unlock..........................65

Fingerprint Sensor 65

Face Unlock..66

   10.2   Software Security Features 67

Secure Operating System 67

Privacy Dashboard 68

Enhanced Permissions Control............................69

Encrypted Data 69

Google Play Protect...70

Conclusion 72

Glossary of Terms for the NUU Mobile A15 76

   A 76

   B 76

   C 77

   D 78

   E..78

   F..79

   G 79

   H 80

   M...80

   O 80

   P..81

   R 81

   S..82

   T..82

U 82
W 83
Appendices 84
Unveiling the Specs: A Deep Dive into the NUU Mobile A15 84
Screen Display 85
   Size and Resolution 85
   Refresh Rate 85
   Brightness and Clarity 86
Processor and RAM 86
   Processor 86
   RAM 87
Internal Storage Options 87
   Storage Capacity 87
Battery Life and Charging Speed 88
   Battery Capacity 88
   Charging Speed 88
Camera Features 89
   Rear Camera 89
   Front Camera 89
Advanced Camera Features 90
Connectivity and Network 90
   Cellular Capabilities 90
   Wi-Fi and Bluetooth 91

GPS and Navigation 91
Expandable Storage 92
Audio and Multimedia 92
    Sound Quality 92
    Media Playback 93
Security and Privacy 93
    Biometric Security 93
    Software Security 94

Maintenance and Troubleshooting 95
Tips for Optimal Performance 95
    Keep Software Updated 95
    Clear Cache and Unnecessary Files 96
    Manage Background Processes 96
    Monitor Battery Health 97
Protect Your Device Physically 97
Common Issues and Solutions 98
    Battery Draining Quickly 98
    Slow Performance 99
    Overheating 100
    Connectivity Issues 101
    App Crashes or Freezes 101
    Unresponsive Screen 102
    Poor Call Quality 103
    Camera Issues 104

Bluetooth Connectivity Problems..105

Phone is Full and Doesn't Allow App Installation................106

Audio Problems 107

Unable to Connect to a Computer 107

Frequently Asked Questions (FAQ) 109

1.0 Introduction

If you're someone who loves to explore new devices or is looking to gift an affordable yet outstanding smartphone, let me introduce you to the NUU A15. Owning this smartphone goes beyond just aesthetics; it boasts powerful configurations meticulously designed with the customer in mind, delivering a device that not only meets but exceeds performance standards.

The NUU A15 is more than just a pretty face. This book will guide you through its exceptional features, from its sleek physical appearance to its robust functionality. We'll delve into every aspect of the NUU A15, ensuring you understand why it's a top contender for anyone seeking a high-quality smartphone.

Whether you're considering an upgrade or searching for a device that can keep up with your high standards and expectations, the NUU A15 is a worthy candidate. Especially for photography enthusiasts, this phone promises to elevate your photo-taking experience.

I can confidently say that this smartphone offers incredible value for its price. If you're ready to explore these amazing features and functions, let's dive in together.

1.1 Why You Need to Choose the NUU A15

Unparalleled Design and Build Quality

The NUU A15 is not just a smartphone; it's a statement. Available in Dark Purple and Pure White, its sleek and minimalist design is a blend of elegance and modern aesthetics. The phone's build quality ensures durability while maintaining a lightweight feel, making it comfortable to hold and use.

Stunning Display

Featuring a 6.5-inch HD+ display with a 90Hz refresh rate, the NUU A15 brings your media to life. Enjoy crystal-clear visuals, vibrant colors, and smooth motion whether you're watching videos, playing games, or browsing the web. This display ensures an immersive viewing experience that's easy on the eyes.

Powerful Performance
At the heart of the NUU A15 is a 2.2GHz octa-core processor, coupled with 4GB of RAM. This combination delivers a seamless and responsive user experience, allowing you to multitask with ease and handle resource-intensive applications without lag. Whether you're gaming, streaming, or working, the A15 is built to perform.

Ample Storage
With 128GB of internal storage, you'll have plenty of space for all your apps, photos, music, and videos. If that's not enough, the NUU A15 supports

expandable storage up to 1TB via microSD, ensuring you never run out of space.

Exceptional Camera System

Capture life's best moments with the NUU A15's advanced dual-camera setup. The 50MP main camera delivers stunningly detailed and vibrant photos, while the VGA Bokeh camera adds depth and artistic flair to your shots. The 5MP front camera ensures your selfies are always picture-perfect. Plus, with AI-enhanced features, your photos will always look their best, regardless of the scene or lighting conditions.

Long-Lasting Battery

The NUU A15 is equipped with a powerful 4,180mAh battery that keeps you connected all day long. Whether you're streaming videos, playing games, or working on the go, you can rely on the A15's battery to keep up with your active lifestyle without the need for frequent recharging.

Advanced Connectivity

Stay connected with 4G LTE support, dual SIM capability, and a wide range of network bands. The NUU A15 also features Wi-Fi 802.11 a/b/g/n/ac for fast internet access, Bluetooth 5.0 for seamless device pairing, and GPS with A-GPS support for accurate navigation.

Enhanced User Experience

Running on Android 13, the NUU A15 offers a customizable and user-friendly interface. Enjoy expanded themed app icons, enhanced media experiences, and customizable language settings, allowing you to tailor your device to your personal preferences.

Security and Convenience

The NUU A15 prioritizes your security with a fingerprint sensor and face unlock features, ensuring your data is protected. These features provide quick and convenient access to your phone, keeping your information secure while being easily accessible.

Excellent Value

With its combination of high-end features, elegant design, and powerful performance, the NUU A15 offers exceptional value for its price. It's a smartphone that doesn't compromise on quality or functionality, making it a smart choice for anyone looking for a reliable and stylish device.

Choose the NUU A15 for a smartphone experience that seamlessly integrates beauty, power, and innovation into your daily life. Whether you're a tech enthusiast, a photography lover, or someone who simply wants a dependable and stylish phone, the NUU A15 is designed to exceed your expectations.

2.0 Unboxing the NUU A15

2.1 First Impressions

Unboxing the NUU A15 is an experience that exudes sophistication and excitement. As you open the sleek, minimalist packaging, the first thing that catches your eye is the beautifully designed device itself. The NUU A15 is nestled securely in a protective sleeve, showcasing its elegant Dark Purple or Pure White finish. The attention to detail in the presentation immediately gives a sense of the quality and thoughtfulness that has gone into this smartphone.

2.2 What's in the Box?

Beneath the NUU A15, you will find an array of accessories and essentials neatly arranged to enhance your user experience. Here's a detailed look at what's included in the box:

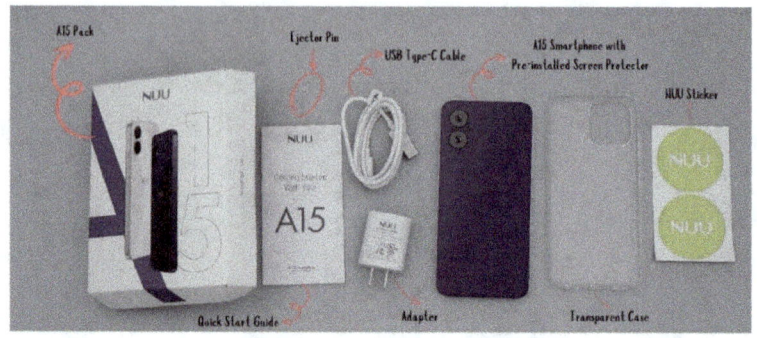

1. **The NUU A15 Device Itself**

    - The NUU A15 smartphone, featuring a stunning 6.5-inch HD+ display, sleek design, and powerful internal specifications, is the centerpiece of the package. As you pick up the device, its lightweight feel and premium finish immediately stand out.

2. **Adapter**

- A compact and efficient adaptor designed to provide fast and reliable charging for your NUU A15. The adaptor ensures your device can quickly recharge, keeping you connected and powered throughout the day.

3. **USB Type-C Cable**

    - A high-quality USB Type-C cable is included for charging and data transfer. The cable's durability and length are designed to offer convenience whether you're at home, in the office, or on the go.

4. **SIM Ejector Tool**

- A handy SIM ejector tool is provided, allowing you to easily access and manage your SIM cards. This tool is essential for setting up your NUU A15 and switching between different SIM cards if needed.

5. **Quick Start User Manual**

    - A comprehensive user manual is included, offering detailed instructions and tips on how to get the most out of your NUU A15. The manual covers everything from initial setup to advanced features, ensuring you can navigate and utilize your new smartphone with ease.

6. **Transparent Pouch**

- A sleek and practical transparent pouch is provided to protect your NUU A15 while showcasing its beautiful design. The pouch offers a layer of protection against scratches and minor impacts, allowing you to maintain the pristine condition of your device.

7. NUU Sticker

3.0 Design and Build Quality

3.1 Sleek and Sophisticated Aesthetics

The NUU A15 stands out with its sleek and sophisticated design, offering a visually appealing experience that catches the eye at first glance. Available in two stunning colors—*Dark Purple and Pure White*—the A15 exudes elegance and modernity. The glossy finish adds a touch of sophistication, making it a device that is both stylish and contemporary.

3.2 Minimalist and Ergonomic Design

The NUU A15 is designed with a minimalist approach, ensuring that every element serves a purpose. The seamless integration of the front and back panels, combined with smooth, rounded edges, provides a comfortable grip, making it easy to hold and use for extended periods. The lightweight build further enhances the ergonomic design, allowing for effortless one-handed use.

3.3 Robust Build Quality

Despite its lightweight and sleek appearance, the NUU A15 is built to last. The device features a durable frame that provides strength and resilience against everyday wear and tear. The robust construction ensures that the phone can withstand minor drops and bumps, offering peace of mind for users with an active lifestyle.

3.4 Premium Materials

The NUU A15 is crafted using high-quality materials that contribute to its premium feel. The use of durable plastics and reinforced glass not only enhances the phone's aesthetic appeal but also ensures long-lasting performance. The materials used are carefully selected to balance durability with a lightweight design, ensuring the phone is both strong and comfortable to use.

3.5 Thoughtful Details

Attention to detail is evident in every aspect of the NUU A15's design. The placement of buttons and ports is meticulously planned for maximum convenience. *The volume rocker and power button are intuitively positioned for easy access, while the USB Type-C port and headphone jack are strategically placed to ensure a clutter-free experience.*

3.6 Display Excellence

The front of the NUU A15 is dominated by its impressive 6.5-inch HD+ display. The slim bezels around the screen maximize the viewing area, providing an immersive visual experience without making the device bulky. The front camera is discreetly placed, ensuring it does not interfere with the overall design harmony.

3.7 Color Options: Dark Purple and Pure White

The NUU A15's color options are carefully chosen to suit different tastes and preferences. The Dark Purple variant exudes a mysterious and luxurious vibe, perfect for those who prefer a bold statement. On the other hand, the Pure White variant offers a clean and timeless look, ideal for users who appreciate simplicity and elegance.

4.0 Display and Experience

4.1 Screen Specifications

6.5" HD+
(90Hz Refresh Rate)

The NUU A15 is equipped with a 6.5-inch HD+ display, offering a resolution of 720 x 1600 pixels. This large screen size provides ample real estate for immersive viewing, whether you're watching videos, playing games, or browsing the web. The 90Hz refresh rate is a standout feature, ensuring smooth motion and reducing blur during fast-paced action scenes or when scrolling through content.

4.2 Visual Clarity and Brightness

One of the most impressive aspects of the NUU A15's display is its visual clarity. The HD+ resolution ensures that images and text are sharp and well-defined, making for an enjoyable viewing experience. Colors are vibrant and lifelike, enhancing the realism of photos and videos. The display also boasts excellent brightness levels, making it easy to see even in bright sunlight. This means you can comfortably use your phone outdoors without struggling to read the screen or view your media.

4.3 Touch Responsiveness

The touch responsiveness of the NUU A15 is exceptional, thanks to its advanced touch technology. The screen is highly responsive to touch inputs, making navigation smooth and intuitive. Whether you're typing a message, swiping through your photo gallery, or playing a game, the screen reacts instantly to your touch. This high level of responsiveness ensures that you can interact with your device effortlessly, enhancing the overall user experience.

4.4 Immersive Viewing Experience

The combination of the large screen size, high resolution, and vibrant color reproduction creates an immersive viewing experience. Whether you're streaming your favorite shows, watching movies, or playing games, the NUU A15's display pulls you into the action. The narrow bezels further enhance this experience by maximizing the screen-to-body ratio, giving you more screen space to enjoy.

4.5 Adaptive Display Features

The NUU A15 comes with adaptive display features that automatically adjust the brightness and color balance based on your environment. This means that the screen remains comfortable to view whether you're in a dark room or under bright sunlight. These adaptive features not only enhance your viewing experience but also help in conserving battery life by optimizing the display settings as needed.

4.6 Eye Comfort Mode

Understanding the importance of reducing eye strain, especially during extended use, the NUU A15 includes an Eye Comfort Mode. This mode reduces blue light emission from the screen, making it easier on your eyes, especially in low-light conditions. Whether you're reading an e-book at night or browsing social media before bed, this feature ensures that your eyes remain comfortable.

5.0 Performance and Hardware

5.1 Processor and RAM

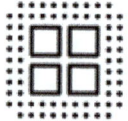

Up to 2.2GHz
Octa-Core

The NUU A15 is powered by a Helio G36 2.2GHz octa-core processor, a robust engine that ensures smooth and efficient performance across all tasks. This powerful processor is designed to handle everything from everyday activities to more demanding applications, such as gaming and multimedia editing. Paired with 4GB of RAM, the NUU A15 offers excellent multitasking capabilities, allowing you to switch between apps seamlessly without experiencing any lag or slowdown. Whether you're browsing the web, streaming videos, or running multiple applications simultaneously, the NUU A15 delivers a fast and responsive user experience.

5.2 Internal Storage Options

When it comes to storage, the NUU A15 offers ample space to accommodate all your digital needs. The device comes with 128GB of internal storage, providing plenty of room for your apps, photos, videos, and documents. For users who require even more storage, the NUU A15 supports expandable storage via a microSD card, allowing you to add up to 1TB of additional space. This flexibility ensures that you will never run out of storage, whether you're a casual user or a digital hoarder who needs to store a large collection of media files.

5.3   Battery Life and Charging Speed

Battery life is a critical aspect of any smartphone, and the NUU A15 excels in this area with its powerful 4,180mAh battery. This high-capacity battery is designed to keep you connected and productive throughout the day. Whether you're streaming videos, playing games, or working on the go, you can rely on the NUU A15 to provide long-lasting power. The efficient power management of the Helio G36 processor also contributes to the device's impressive battery performance, ensuring that you get the most out of each charge.

In addition to its long battery life, the NUU A15 supports fast charging, allowing you to quickly recharge your device and get back to your activities. The included adaptor and USB Type-C cable facilitate rapid charging, so you spend less time tethered to an outlet and more time enjoying your phone. This combination of a high-capacity battery and fast charging capabilities ensures that the NUU A15 can keep up with even the most demanding users.

6.0   Software and User Interface

Operating System Overview

The NUU A15 runs on Android 13, the latest version of Google's widely acclaimed operating system. Android 13 brings a host of improvements and new features designed to enhance user experience, boost performance, and offer greater customization options. With a focus on user-centric design, Android 13 ensures that your NUU A15 is both intuitive and powerful, providing a seamless and enjoyable experience from the moment you turn it on.

6.1 Key Features and Customizations

Expanded Themed App Icons

One of the standout features of Android 13 is the expanded themed app icons. This feature allows you to customize the appearance of your app icons to match your phone's wallpaper tint and colors, extending beyond Google apps to include many third-party apps. This level of customization ensures that your NUU A15 looks and feels uniquely yours, with a cohesive and visually appealing aesthetic.

Enhanced Media Experience

Android 13 introduces a new media player that highlights album artwork and features a dynamic playback bar, enhancing your media consumption experience. Whether you're listening to music, watching videos, or streaming content, the media player provides an engaging and immersive experience, making it easier to control playback and enjoy your favorite media.

Customizable Language Settings

For multilingual users, Android 13 offers the ability to assign different language settings to individual apps. This feature allows you to seamlessly switch between languages based on the app you're using, providing a more personalized and user-friendly experience. Whether you're chatting with friends, browsing the web, or using productivity apps, you can effortlessly navigate your preferred languages.

Privacy and Security Enhancements

Android 13 places a strong emphasis on privacy and security, introducing features such as a new privacy dashboard that provides a clear overview of how apps access your data. Additionally, enhanced permissions controls give you greater control over which apps can access sensitive information, ensuring that your data remains secure and your privacy is protected.

Pre-installed Applications

The NUU A15 comes with a selection of pre-installed applications designed to enhance your productivity and entertainment. These apps are carefully chosen to provide essential functionality while ensuring that your device remains clutter-free and efficient.

Google Suite

The NUU A15 includes a full suite of Google applications, such as Gmail, Google Maps, Google Photos, and Google Drive. These apps provide seamless integration with your Google account, allowing you to access your emails, navigate with ease, manage your photos, and store files in the cloud. The Google Suite ensures that you have all the tools you need for communication, navigation, and productivity right at your fingertips.

Essential Utilities

In addition to Google apps, the NUU A15 features essential utilities such as a calendar, calculator, clock, and weather app. These utilities are designed to help you manage your daily activities, stay organized, and keep track of important events and appointments.

NUU-Specific Applications

The NUU A15 also comes with a few proprietary applications that enhance the overall user experience. These may include a custom camera app with advanced features and settings, a file manager for organizing your files, and a system optimizer to keep your device running smoothly.

Minimal Bloatware

NUU Mobile has taken care to ensure that the A15 is free from unnecessary bloatware. This approach not only provides a cleaner and more efficient user experience but also ensures that you have more storage space available for the apps and content that matter most to you.

7.0 Camera and Network

7.1. Camera Specifications

The NUU A15 boasts a robust dual-camera setup designed to capture stunning photos and videos with exceptional clarity and detail. Here are the key specifications:

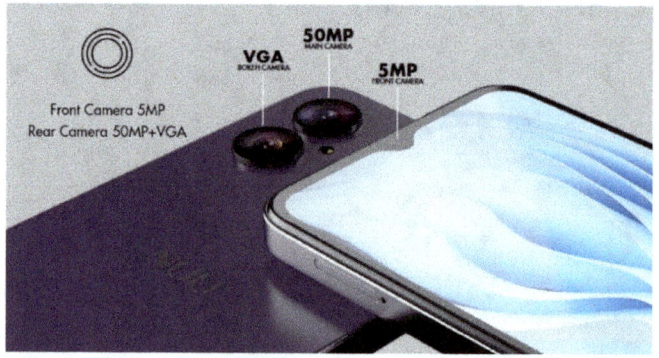

- **Main Rear Camera**: 50MP with Auto Focus (AF)

- **Secondary Rear Camera**: VGA Bokeh camera for depth effects

- **Front Camera**: 5MP for selfies and video calls

These cameras are supported by advanced AI capabilities that enhance image quality and provide a range of creative options for photography enthusiasts.

7.2 Photo and Video Quality

7.2.1 Rear Camera Performance

The 50MP main rear camera on the NUU A15 is designed to capture high-resolution images with excellent detail and vibrant colors. Whether you're photographing landscapes, portraits, or everyday moments, this camera ensures that every shot is sharp and lifelike. The VGA Bokeh camera adds a professional touch by creating a beautiful depth-of-field effect, making your subjects stand out against blurred backgrounds.

In low-light conditions, the NUU A15 excels with its advanced sensor and image processing capabilities, which reduce noise and enhance clarity. This means you can capture great photos even in challenging lighting situations.

7.2.2   Front Camera Performance

The 5MP front camera is perfect for selfies and video calls. It delivers clear and vibrant images, ensuring that your self-portraits look their best.

Whether you're taking a quick selfie or engaging in a video chat with friends and family, the front camera provides high-quality visuals.

7.2.3 Video Quality

The NUU A15 is capable of recording high-definition video, ensuring that your memories are captured in stunning detail. The camera's video stabilization feature helps to reduce shake, resulting in smoother and more professional-looking footage. Whether you're recording a family event or capturing a scenic view, the NUU A15's video capabilities ensure excellent quality.

7.3 Advanced Camera Features

7.3.1 AI Camera Modes

The NUU A15's AI-enhanced camera system intelligently recognizes different scenes and objects, automatically adjusting settings to optimize image quality. Whether you're shooting a portrait, landscape, or a close-up of your pet, the AI camera ensures that every photo looks its best. This feature simplifies the photography process, allowing you to focus on capturing the moment rather than adjusting settings.

7.3.2   Pro Mode

For photography enthusiasts who want more control over their shots, the NUU A15 offers a Pro Mode. This mode allows you to manually adjust settings such as ISO, aperture, and shutter speed, giving you the flexibility to capture photos just the way you envision them. Whether you're experimenting with long exposures or fine-tuning the focus, Pro Mode provides the tools you need for creative photography.

7.3.3 Selfie Enhancements

The front camera includes a variety of enhancements specifically designed for selfies. Features like beauty mode, which smooths skin tones and adjusts lighting, ensure that your selfies always look their best. Additionally, the camera supports various filters and effects, allowing you to add a personal touch to your photos.

7.4 Network

7.4.1 Connectivity Options

The NUU A15 is equipped with a comprehensive set of connectivity options, ensuring that you stay connected wherever you go. Key features include:

- **4G LTE**: Fast and reliable mobile data connectivity for seamless browsing, streaming, and downloading.

4G LTE

- **Wi-Fi 802.11 a/b/g/n/ac**: Dual-band Wi-Fi support (2.4GHz and 5GHz) for high-speed internet access at home, work, or public hotspots.

- **Bluetooth 5.0**: Efficient and stable wireless connections for peripherals like headphones, speakers, and smartwatches.

- **GPS with A-GPS Support**: Accurate location tracking and navigation capabilities for driving, walking, and outdoor activities.

- **USB Type-C 2.0**: Versatile port for charging, data transfer, and connecting various accessories.

7.4.2 Dual SIM Capability

Dual SIM

The NUU A15 supports dual SIM functionality, allowing you to use two different phone numbers simultaneously. This is particularly useful for users who want to separate personal and professional calls or for travelers who need to use a local SIM card while keeping their home number active. The dual SIM feature offers flexibility and convenience, making it easier to manage multiple connections.

7.4.3   Expandable Storage

microSD
(up to 1TB)

While the NUU A15 comes with a generous 128GB of internal storage, it also supports expandable storage via a microSD card. You can add up to 1TB of additional storage, providing ample space for your photos, videos, music, and apps. This expandable storage option ensures that you never run out of space, giving you the flexibility to store all your important data without worrying about limitations. Whether you need extra room for high-resolution media files or large applications, the NUU A15 has you covered.

8.0 Audio and Multimedia

8.1 Sound Quality and Speaker Performance

Sound Quality

The NUU A15 delivers a superior audio experience, designed to satisfy even the most discerning listeners. Its advanced sound technology ensures that audio playback is crisp, clear, and immersive. Whether you're listening to music, watching movies, or playing games, the NUU A15 provides rich and detailed sound quality that enhances your overall multimedia experience.

Speaker Performance

The NUU A15 is equipped with high-quality speakers that offer robust performance for all your audio needs. The speakers deliver balanced sound with a good mix of highs, mids, and lows, ensuring that you can enjoy your favorite content without distortion, even at higher volumes. The clarity and depth of the audio make it ideal for various uses, from casual listening to more intensive multimedia consumption. Additionally, the phone's built-in equalizer allows you to customize the audio settings to match your personal preferences, further enhancing the listening experience.

8.2   Media Playback Features

Enhanced Media Experience

The NUU A15's 6.5-inch HD+ display with a 90Hz refresh rate is perfect for media playback, providing stunning visual clarity and smooth motion. Combined with the phone's superior sound quality, the NUU A15 offers an immersive media experience that brings your favorite content to life. Whether you're streaming movies, binge-watching series, or enjoying online videos, the high-resolution display and excellent audio quality make every viewing session a pleasure.

Versatile Media Support

The NUU A15 supports a wide range of audio and video formats, ensuring compatibility with various types of media files. This versatility means you can enjoy your favorite content without worrying about format restrictions. The device's powerful processor and ample RAM ensure smooth playback, even for high-definition videos and resource-intensive applications.

Streaming and Connectivity

With its robust connectivity options, the NUU A15 makes streaming content from your favorite platforms easy and convenient. The device supports fast 4G LTE and dual-band Wi-Fi, providing stable and high-speed internet connections for uninterrupted streaming. Whether you're using services like Netflix, YouTube, or Spotify, the NUU A15 ensures that you can access your favorite content quickly and reliably.

Audio Enhancements and Customizations

The NUU A15 comes with several audio enhancement features that allow you to tailor the sound to your liking. Features such as Dolby Atmos support and built-in equalizer settings provide options to enhance the audio output, whether you prefer deep bass, clear vocals, or balanced sound. These customizations ensure that you can enjoy your media the way you want to, with sound settings that match your preferences.

10.0 Security and Privacy

Ensuring the safety of your data and maintaining your privacy are paramount concerns in today's digital age. The NUU A15 is equipped with robust security and privacy features designed to protect your personal information and provide peace of mind. This chapter delves into the advanced security measures of the NUU A15, focusing on the fingerprint sensor, face unlock technology, and software security features.

10.1 Fingerprint Sensor and Face Unlock

<u>Fingerprint Sensor</u>

The NUU A15 includes a highly responsive fingerprint sensor that offers quick and secure access to your device. Located conveniently on the back of the phone, the fingerprint sensor allows you to unlock your device with just a touch. The sensor is designed to be highly accurate, reducing the chances of false rejections and ensuring that only your fingerprint can unlock the phone. This biometric security feature provides a fast, reliable, and secure way to access your phone, making it difficult for unauthorized users to gain entry.

Face Unlock

In addition to the fingerprint sensor, the NUU A15 also features face unlock technology. This feature uses the front camera to scan your face and unlock the device instantly. Face unlock provides a convenient and secure method for accessing your phone, especially when your hands are occupied.

The technology employs advanced algorithms to recognize your facial features accurately, ensuring that it cannot be easily fooled by photos or other images. The combination of face unlock and fingerprint sensor adds an extra layer of security, giving you multiple options for securing your device.

10.2 Software Security Features

<u>Secure Operating System</u>

The NUU A15 runs on Android 13, which includes numerous security enhancements to protect your device and personal data. Android 13 introduces a range of new security features and improvements over previous versions, ensuring that your phone is safeguarded against the latest threats. The operating system includes regular security updates from Google, which address vulnerabilities and provide patches to keep your device secure.

Privacy Dashboard

One of the standout features of Android 13 is the Privacy Dashboard. This tool provides a comprehensive overview of how your data is being used by different apps. You can see which apps have accessed your location, camera, microphone, and other sensitive data over the past 24 hours. The Privacy Dashboard allows you to manage permissions easily, giving you greater control over your data and ensuring that apps only access the information they need.

Enhanced Permissions Control

Android 13 offers improved permissions controls, allowing you to grant one-time permissions to apps for accessing sensitive data like location, microphone, and camera. This means that apps can only access these features when you explicitly allow them, reducing the risk of unauthorized data access. Additionally, the operating system will notify you if an app accesses sensitive data in the background, helping you stay informed about how your information is being used.

Encrypted Data

The NUU A15 includes robust encryption protocols to protect your data. Encryption ensures that your data is converted into a secure format that can only be read by authorized parties. This is especially important for protecting sensitive information such as personal documents, photos, and financial details. With encryption, even if your device falls into the wrong hands, your data remains secure and inaccessible.

Google Play Protect

Google Play Protect is integrated into the NUU A15, providing an additional layer of security. This feature scans apps for malware and other threats before you download them from the Google Play Store. Play Protect also continuously monitors your device for harmful apps, offering real-time protection against malware and phishing attacks. If a potentially harmful app is detected, Play

Protect will alert you and provide options to remove the threat.

Conclusion

The NUU Mobile A15 stands out as a compelling choice in the competitive smartphone market, blending style, performance, and affordability into one sleek package. Its impressive 6.5-inch HD+ display, complemented by a 90Hz refresh rate, offers a visually stunning and smooth user experience, perfect for enjoying multimedia content and seamless app interactions. The design of the A15, available in elegant Dark Purple and Pure White, adds a touch of sophistication, making it not only a device but also a fashion statement.

Under the hood, the A15 is powered by a Helio G36 octa-core processor clocked at 2.2GHz and 4GB of RAM, ensuring smooth performance whether you're multitasking, gaming, or running demanding applications. The generous 128GB of internal storage, expandable up to 1TB with a microSD card, provides ample space for all your photos, videos, apps, and other media. This means you'll never have to worry about running out of storage space.

Battery life is another strong suit of the NUU Mobile A15. Its 4,180mAh battery ensures you can stay connected and productive throughout the day without constantly reaching for a charger. Coupled with efficient power management, the

A15 offers reliable performance for all your daily activities.

Photography enthusiasts will appreciate the advanced camera capabilities of the A15. The 50MP main camera captures stunningly detailed and vibrant images, while the 5MP front camera is perfect for clear and crisp selfies and video calls. The AI camera features and Pro Mode offer additional tools to enhance your photography, making every shot a masterpiece.

Connectivity is robust with the A15, supporting 4G LTE, dual SIM functionality, Wi-Fi 802.11 a/b/g/n/ac, and Bluetooth 5.0, ensuring you stay connected wherever you go. The inclusion of a fingerprint sensor and face unlock provides quick and secure access to your device, while Android 13 offers the latest software features and security updates to keep your data safe and your experience seamless.

The NUU Mobile A15 is a versatile and powerful smartphone that caters to a wide range of needs. Whether you're a power user, a photography lover, or someone who values elegant design, the A15 delivers a comprehensive and satisfying mobile experience. With its combination of advanced features, robust performance, and stylish design, the NUU Mobile A15 is poised to become your next favorite smartphone.

Glossary of Terms for the NUU Mobile A15

A

- **AI Camera**: A camera system that uses artificial intelligence to recognize different scenes and objects, optimizing settings for the best possible shot.

- **Android 13**: The operating system running on the NUU Mobile A15, offering various features, security enhancements, and customization options.

B

- **Battery Capacity**: The amount of charge a battery can hold, measured in milliampere-hours (mAh). The A15 has a 4,180mAh battery.

- **Bluetooth 5.0**: A version of Bluetooth technology that offers improved speed, range, and data transfer capabilities.

C

- **Cellular Connectivity**: The ability of the device to connect to mobile networks for voice and data services. The A15 supports 4G LTE, 3G, and 2G networks.

- **Camera Resolution**: The amount of detail a camera can capture, measured in megapixels (MP). The A15 features a 50MP main camera and a 5MP front camera.

D

- **Dual SIM**: The capability to use two SIM cards in one device, allowing for two different phone numbers or carriers to be used simultaneously.

- **Display Resolution**: The number of pixels on the screen, which determines the clarity and detail of the display. The A15 has a resolution of 720 x 1600 pixels.

E

- **Expandable Storage**: The ability to increase the device's storage capacity using external memory cards. The A15 supports microSD cards up to 1TB.

F

- **Fingerprint Sensor**: A biometric security feature that uses your fingerprint to unlock the device.

- **Front Camera**: The camera located on the front of the device, used primarily for selfies and video calls. The A15 has a 5MP front camera.

G

- **GPS (Global Positioning System)**: A navigation system that uses satellite signals to determine the device's location. The A15 includes GPS with A-GPS support.

H

- **HD+**: High Definition Plus, a display resolution that offers better quality than standard HD. The A15's screen is HD+.

M

- **microSD Card**: A type of removable flash memory card used for storing additional data. The A15 supports microSD cards for expandable storage.

O

- **Octa-Core Processor**: A processor with eight cores, allowing for better multitasking and performance. The A15 uses a Helio G36 octa-core processor.

P

- **Pro Mode**: A camera setting that allows manual control over camera parameters such as ISO, aperture, and shutter speed.

- **Processor Speed**: The speed at which a processor operates, measured in gigahertz (GHz). The A15's processor runs up to 2.2GHz.

R

- **RAM (Random Access Memory)**: The memory used by the device to run applications and multitask. The A15 has 4GB of RAM.

- **Refresh Rate**: The number of times the display updates per second, measured in hertz (Hz). The A15 has a 90Hz refresh rate.

S

- **SIM Card**: Subscriber Identity Module, a card that stores user data for cellular service. The A15 supports dual SIM cards.

- **Storage Capacity**: The amount of internal memory available for storing data. The A15 has 128GB of internal storage.

T

- **Touch Responsiveness**: How quickly and accurately the screen responds to touch inputs.

U

- **USB Type-C**: A type of USB connector that is reversible and supports faster data transfer and charging. The A15 uses a USB Type-C port.

W

- **Wi-Fi 802.11 a/b/g/n/ac**: The wireless networking standards supported by the device, allowing for various Wi-Fi connections. The A15 supports both 2.4GHz and 5GHz bands.

Appendices

Unveiling the Specs: A Deep Dive into the NUU Mobile A15

The NUU Mobile A15 is a device that combines aesthetics with powerful performance, designed to meet the diverse needs of modern smartphone users. This chapter provides a detailed examination of the NUU Mobile A15's specifications, highlighting its screen display, processing power, storage capabilities, battery life, camera features, connectivity options, and more.

Screen Display

Size and Resolution

- **Display Size**: The NUU Mobile A15 features a 6.5-inch display, providing ample screen real estate for a comfortable viewing experience.

- **Resolution**: With an HD+ resolution of 720 x 1600 pixels, the A15 offers sharp and clear visuals, making it suitable for watching videos, browsing the web, and gaming.

Refresh Rate

- **90Hz Refresh Rate**: The 90Hz refresh rate ensures smoother scrolling and more responsive touch interactions, enhancing the overall user experience by reducing motion blur and making animations appear more fluid.

Brightness and Clarity

- **Brightness**: The display is designed to be bright enough to be used comfortably in various lighting conditions, including direct sunlight.

- **Visual Clarity**: The combination of HD+ resolution and high brightness levels ensures that text and images are crisp and easy to read.

Processor and RAM

Processor

- **Helio G36 Octa-Core Processor**: The NUU Mobile A15 is powered by a Helio G36 octa-core processor clocked at 2.2GHz. This processor provides the necessary power to handle multitasking, gaming, and other demanding applications with ease.

RAM

- **4GB RAM**: With 4GB of RAM, the A15 offers smooth performance and efficient multitasking capabilities, allowing users to switch between apps without experiencing significant lag.

Internal Storage Options

Storage Capacity

- **128GB Internal Storage**: The A15 comes with 128GB of internal storage, providing ample space for apps, photos, videos, and other media.

- **Expandable Storage**: The device supports microSD cards up to 1TB, allowing users to expand their storage capacity as needed.

Battery Life and Charging Speed

Battery Capacity

- **4,180mAh Battery**: The NUU Mobile A15 is equipped with a 4,180mAh battery, designed to provide long-lasting performance throughout the day. Whether you're streaming videos, playing games, or browsing the web, the battery is built to keep up with your demands.

Charging Speed

- **Standard Charging**: While the A15 does not support fast charging, its efficient battery management ensures that you can quickly get back to using your phone after plugging it in for a charge.

Camera Features

Rear Camera

- **50MP Main Camera**: The primary camera on the NUU Mobile A15 is a 50MP sensor that captures high-resolution images with vibrant colors and sharp details.

- **VGA Secondary Camera**: This secondary camera supports additional photography modes and enhances the primary camera's capabilities, especially in portrait and low-light settings.

Front Camera
- **5MP Front Camera**: The front-facing camera is a 5MP sensor that ensures your selfies are clear and detailed, and it also supports high-quality video calls.

Advanced Camera Features
- **AI Camera Modes**: The AI-powered camera system can recognize different scenes and

objects, optimizing settings for the best possible shot. This includes modes for portraits, landscapes, and pet photography.

- **Pro Mode**: For users who want more control over their photography, Pro Mode allows manual adjustments to settings such as ISO, aperture, and shutter speed.

Connectivity and Network

Cellular Capabilities

- **4G LTE**: The NUU Mobile A15 supports 4G LTE networks, ensuring fast and reliable internet connectivity.

- **Dual SIM**: The device features dual SIM capabilities, allowing you to manage two phone numbers simultaneously, which is ideal for separating personal and work contacts.

Wi-Fi and Bluetooth

- **Wi-Fi**: The A15 supports Wi-Fi 802.11 a/b/g/n/ac on both 2.4GHz and 5GHz bands, providing robust wireless connectivity options.

- **Bluetooth 5.0**: With Bluetooth 5.0, the A15 offers enhanced data transfer speeds and improved range for connecting peripherals such as headphones, speakers, and other devices.

GPS and Navigation

- **GPS with A-GPS Support**: The device includes GPS functionality with A-GPS support, ensuring accurate location tracking and reliable navigation services.

Expandable Storage
- **microSD Card Slot**: The microSD card slot supports expandable storage up to 1TB, providing flexibility for users who need additional space for their files and media.

Audio and Multimedia
Sound Quality
- **Speaker Performance**: The A15 is equipped with a quality speaker that delivers clear and loud audio, making it suitable for media playback and hands-free calls.

- **3.5mm Headphone Jack**: The inclusion of a 3.5mm headphone jack allows users to connect wired headphones for a traditional audio experience.

Media Playback

- **High-Definition Playback**: The device supports high-definition media playback, ensuring that videos and music sound and look great.

- **Built-in FM Radio**: For users who enjoy live radio, the A15 includes a built-in FM radio feature.

Security and Privacy

Biometric Security

- **Fingerprint Sensor**: The rear-mounted fingerprint sensor provides quick and secure access to your device.

- **Face Unlock**: The front camera supports face unlock, adding an additional layer of security.

Software Security

- **Android 13**: The NUU Mobile A15 runs on Android 13, which includes the latest security features and regular updates to protect your data.

- **Privacy Dashboard**: Android 13's Privacy Dashboard gives users control over app permissions and data access, enhancing overall privacy.

Maintenance and Troubleshooting

Ensuring your smartphone remains in optimal working condition requires regular maintenance and the ability to troubleshoot common issues effectively. In this chapter, we will provide tips for maintaining peak performance and outline solutions for common problems that users may encounter with their smartphones.

Tips for Optimal Performance

Keep Software Updated

Regularly updating your smartphone's operating system and apps ensures that you have the latest features, security patches, and performance improvements. Check for updates periodically in the settings menu and install them as soon as they become available.

Clear Cache and Unnecessary Files

Over time, cache and temporary files can accumulate, slowing down your device. Regularly clear cache from your apps and delete unnecessary files. You can use built-in tools like "Storage" in settings or third-party apps designed for cleaning and optimizing your device.

Manage Background Processes

Apps running in the background can drain your battery and reduce performance. Use the task manager to close unnecessary background apps and disable auto-start for apps that don't need to run constantly.

[Monitor Battery Health](#)

To prolong battery life, avoid letting your phone's battery drain completely or charging it to 100% all the time. Use features like Battery Saver mode when you're low on power and monitor your battery usage in the settings to identify power-hungry apps.

Protect Your Device Physically

Use a protective case and screen protector to shield your phone from physical damage. Avoid exposing your device to extreme temperatures, moisture, and dust to keep it functioning well.

Common Issues and Solutions

Battery Draining Quickly

Solution

- **Identify Power-Hungry Apps**: Check your battery usage in settings to see which apps consume the most power. Uninstall or limit the use of these apps.

- **Reduce Screen Brightness**: Lowering the screen brightness can significantly save battery life.

- **Disable Unnecessary Features**: Turn off features like Bluetooth, Wi-Fi, and GPS when not in use.

- **Enable Battery Saver Mode**: This mode helps extend battery life by limiting background processes and reducing performance.

Slow Performance
Solution

- **Free Up Storage**: Delete unnecessary files, apps, and media to free up storage space.

- **Clear Cache**: Regularly clear the cache of your apps.

- **Restart Your Phone**: A simple restart can sometimes resolve performance issues.

- **Update Software**: Ensure that your phone's operating system and apps are up to date.

Overheating

Solution

- **Remove Case**: If your phone is overheating, try removing its case to allow better heat dissipation.

- **Close Background Apps**: Close apps running in the background that might be causing the device to heat up.

- **Avoid Intensive Tasks**: Give your phone a break from resource-intensive tasks like gaming or video streaming if it's overheating.

- **Cool Down**: Turn off your phone and let it cool down in a shaded, cool place.

Connectivity Issues

Solution

- **Restart Phone**: Restart your phone to reset network connections.

- **Toggle Airplane Mode**: Turn on Airplane Mode for a few seconds and then turn it off to refresh network connections.

- **Forget and Reconnect to Wi-Fi**: For Wi-Fi issues, forget the network and reconnect.

- **Reset Network Settings**: If issues persist, reset your network settings in the settings menu.

App Crashes or Freezes

Solution

- **Update the App**: Ensure the app is updated to the latest version.

- **Clear App Cache**: Go to the app settings and clear the cache.

- **Reinstall the App**: Uninstall the app and then reinstall it from the app store.

- **Check for System Updates**: Sometimes, an outdated operating system can cause app compatibility issues.

Unresponsive Screen
Solution

- **Clean the Screen**: Ensure the screen is clean and free of dirt and debris.

- **Restart Phone**: A restart can sometimes fix an unresponsive screen.

- **Safe Mode**: Boot your phone in safe mode to determine if a third-party app is causing the issue.

- **Factory Reset**: As a last resort, perform a factory reset after backing up your data.

Poor Call Quality
Solution

- **Check Signal Strength**: Ensure you have a good signal. Move to an area with better coverage if necessary.

- **Remove Case**: Sometimes, cases can interfere with signal reception.

- **Reset Network Settings**: Reset your network settings to resolve any configuration issues.

- **Update Carrier Settings**: Ensure your phone's carrier settings are up to date.

Camera Issues
Solution

- **Clean the Lens**: Make sure the camera lens is clean and free of smudges.

- **Restart Camera App**: Close and restart the camera app.

- **Check for Updates**: Ensure the camera app and phone software are up to date.

- **Reset Camera Settings**: Reset the camera settings to default.

Bluetooth Connectivity Problems
Solution

- **Restart Bluetooth**: Turn Bluetooth off and back on.

- **Re-pair Devices**: Forget the Bluetooth device and pair it again.

- **Check Compatibility**: Ensure both devices are compatible.

- **Reset Network Settings**: Resetting network settings can also resolve Bluetooth issues.

Phone is Full and Doesn't Allow App Installation
Solution

- **Delete Unnecessary Files and Apps**: Remove apps and files that you no longer need.

- **Move Files to External Storage**: Use a microSD card to store media files and free up internal storage.

- **Clear App Data and Cache**: Go to the settings and clear the cache and data of apps that are using a lot of storage.

- **Use Cloud Storage**: Move photos, videos, and other large files to cloud storage services to free up space on your device.

Audio Problems
Solution

- **Check Volume Settings**: Ensure the volume is not muted and is set to an appropriate level.

- **Clean Speaker and Headphone Jack**: Remove any dust or debris from the speaker grills and headphone jack.

- **Restart the Phone**: Restart your device to resolve temporary audio glitches.

- **Test with Headphones**: Use headphones to check if the issue is with the speaker or the audio output system.

Unable to Connect to a Computer
Solution

- **Check USB Cable and Port**: Ensure that the USB cable and port are not damaged.

- **Enable USB Debugging**: Turn on USB debugging in the developer options in settings.

- **Select Proper USB Mode**: When connecting, choose the appropriate USB connection mode, such as "File Transfer" or "MTP."

- **Update Drivers**: Ensure that your computer has the latest USB drivers installed for your smartphone.

Frequently Asked Questions (FAQ)

> ➢ **General Solution**

Q1: What colors is the NUU Mobile A15 available in?

The NUU Mobile A15 is available in two stunning colors: Dark Purple and Pure White.

Q2: What is the price of the NUU Mobile A15?

Pricing may vary depending on the region and retailer. It's best to check the official NUU Mobile website or authorized retailers for the latest pricing information.

> ➢ **Display and Design**

Q3: What is the display size and resolution of the NUU Mobile A15?

The NUU Mobile A15 features a 6.5-inch HD+ display with a resolution of 720 x 1600 pixels.

Q4: Does the NUU Mobile A15 have a high refresh rate?

Yes, the A15 has a 90Hz refresh rate, which provides smoother scrolling and a more responsive touch experience.

➢ **Performance and Hardware**

Q5: What processor does the NUU Mobile A15 use?

The A15 is powered by a Helio G36 octa-core processor clocked at 2.2GHz.

Q6: How much RAM and internal storage does the NUU Mobile A15 have?

The A15 comes with 4GB of RAM and 128GB of internal storage, which can be expanded up to 1TB with a microSD card.

➢ **Battery and Charging**

Q7: What is the battery capacity of the NUU Mobile A15?

The NUU Mobile A15 is equipped with a 4,180mAh battery.

Q8: Does the NUU Mobile A15 support fast charging?

No, the A15 does not support fast charging but offers efficient battery management for prolonged use.

➢ **Camera Features**

Q9: What are the camera specifications of the NUU Mobile A15?

The rear camera setup includes a 50MP main sensor and a VGA secondary sensor. The front camera is a 5MP sensor.

Q10: Does the NUU Mobile A15 have advanced camera features?

Yes, the A15 features AI camera modes and a Pro Mode for manual adjustments. It also includes various scene optimizations for better photo quality.

> **Connectivity and Network**

Q11: What network bands does the NUU Mobile A15 support?

The A15 supports various 4G LTE bands, as well as 3G and 2G bands, providing wide coverage and reliable connectivity.

Q12: Does the NUU Mobile A15 support dual SIM functionality?

Yes, the A15 supports dual SIM cards, allowing users to manage two phone numbers simultaneously.

Q13: What Wi-Fi and Bluetooth versions does the NUU Mobile A15 support?

The A15 supports Wi-Fi 802.11 a/b/g/n/ac on both 2.4GHz and 5GHz bands and Bluetooth 5.0.

> **Software and User Interface**

Q14: What operating system does the NUU Mobile A15 run on?

The NUU Mobile A15 runs on Android 13.

Q15: Are there any pre-installed applications on the NUU Mobile A15?

Yes, the A15 comes with several pre-installed applications, including Google apps and other essential utilities.

➢ **Security and Privacy**

Q16: What biometric security features does the NUU Mobile A15 offer?

The A15 includes a rear-mounted fingerprint sensor and face unlock for quick and secure access.

Q17: What software security features are included in the NUU Mobile A15?

The A15 benefits from Android 13's security features, including the Privacy Dashboard and regular security updates.

➢ **Troubleshooting and Maintenance**

Q18: What should I do if my NUU Mobile A15 is running slow?

You can try clearing the cache, freeing up storage space, closing background apps, and ensuring your software is up to date. Restarting the device can also help.

Q19: How can I resolve connectivity issues on my NUU Mobile A15?

Restart your phone, toggle Airplane Mode on and off, forget and reconnect to Wi-Fi networks, and reset network settings if necessary.

Q20: What steps should I take if my NUU Mobile A15's battery drains quickly?

Identify and manage power-hungry apps, reduce screen brightness, disable unnecessary features, and use Battery Saver mode.

> ➤ **Purchasing and Support**

Q21: Where can I buy the NUU Mobile A15?

The NUU Mobile A15 can be purchased from the official NUU Mobile website, authorized online retailers, and select brick-and-mortar stores.

Q22: What is the warranty period for the NUU Mobile A15?

The warranty period may vary by region. Check the warranty information provided at the time of purchase or consult NUU Mobile's customer support for details.

www.ingramcontent.com/pod-product-compliance
Lightning Source LLC
Chambersburg PA
CBHW050109230526
45470CB00004B/1753